Feb 2010.

from Stephen, Jo. Freddie + Vanessa.

SWALEDALE

SWALEDALE

Roly Smith with Photographs by Mike Kipling

F
FRANCES LINCOLN LIMITED
PUBLISHERS

Frances Lincoln Ltd
4 Torriano Mews
Torriano Avenue
London NW5 2RZ
www.franceslincoln.com

British Library Cataloguing-in-Publication data
A catalogue record for this book is available from the British Library.

ISBN 13: 978-0-7112-2636-4
ISBN 10: 0-7112-2636-9

Printed and bound in Singapore

9 8 7 6 5 4 3 2 1

above
The settlements in Arkengarthdale are scattered
and isolated, as in most of Swaledale.

half title page
Healaugh sits in a network of drystone walls,
with the heather covered heights of Calver Hill
beyond.

title page
This is many peoples' favourite view in the whole
of the Yorkshire Dales, let alone Swaledale. The
amusingly-named Crackpot Hall, now ruinous,
stands at the end of a steep track above the
junction of Swinner Gill with the Swale. This
view looks south towards Muker, with the slopes
of Black Hill on the left.

CONTENTS

SWALEDALE: THE WILD ONE

Swaledale is my favourite Yorkshire dale, but then I admit I'm biased. This wildest and northernmost of the Dales was my introduction to the hills of northern England nearly 50 years ago, and will therefore always hold a special place in my memory.

We were on a school youth hostelling holiday from the flatlands of East Anglia, most of us heading north for the first time in our young lives. As our coach swung off the Great North Road, as the A1(M) used to be more romantically known, and entered the perfect, castle-crowned and cobbled market town of Richmond, the horizon of hills started to close in.

The coach carried us on up the winding valley road, past exciting, northern-sounding villages like Applegarth, Marske and Marrick, and my nose was pressed against the steamy window glass as the hills on either side seemed to get higher and higher. Eventually we entered the pretty, stone-built village of Grinton and turned up what seemed to be an impossibly-steep and narrow by-road which led us to the castellated pile of Grinton Lodge Youth Hostel, high on its shelf overlooking the dale.

I can still vividly remember the hardly-contained sense of excitement we felt as the coach pulled up. We'd never seen anything like this before, and the thought that we would actually be staying in this mock-Gothic, fairy-tale castle in the heart of these imposing hills was exhilarating. I remember we all tumbled out of the coach and immediately started to roll stones down into Cogden Gill below, before being restrained by our geography teacher.

Of course, I've been back many times since, and although the hills may have lost some of that virginal awesomeness, I still feel that buzz of excitement when I leave Richmond and head west up the dale, through the fields and barns which make Swaledale and its northern neighbour, Arkengarthdale, perhaps the most archetypal and beautiful of the Yorkshire Dales.

Scarborough-born photographer Mike Kipling's love of Swaledale was kindled during the time when he was an Assistant Area Planning

Buttercups and barns near Muker.

A classic view of walls and barns near Thwaite.

Officer at Richmond, his first job after qualifying at Newcastle University. This was his initial introduction to the Dales, and Wensleydale, south Teesdale and Swaledale became his local patch.

As a newly qualified planner, his role was dealing with minor planning proposals for developments like garages, porches and barn extensions. But two or three times a week, he would travel up one dale or the other in his trusty green Vauxhall Viva doing site reports. Looking back, Mike is sure that his was when he first fell in love with the Dales.

Although he moved on from the post after 18 months, his deep affection for Richmond and Swaledale in particular has always stayed with him, as his magnificent photographs in this volume testify.

* * *

There are few scenes more instantly-recognisably as English than the view down Swaledale from the moors above. I have in mind the view looking north towards Muker from Hill Top, on the old bridleway above Gun Ing Lane. The compact grey village, dominated by the tower of its medieval church, seems to grow almost organically from the native bedrock. It sits like a spider at the centre of an intricate web of drystone walls spreading up the slopes of Kisdon and Muker Side above. Every couple of enclosed meadows seems to have their own little gabled barn ready to take the summer's harvest of sweet-smelling, herb-rich hay.

That harmonious blending of the work of Man and Nature – the lush, alder-lined flood meadows rich in wildflowers; the grey-stone villages clustered around an ancient arched birdge; then one stone barn to every two drystone-walled fields as the slopes rear up to the crags and moorland heights above – is nowhere seen to better effect than in Swaledale.

Proud Yorkshireman JB Preistley wrote: "In all my travels I've never seen a countryside to equal in beauty the Yorkshire Dales." And local walker and author Alfred J Brown went even further: "It is a landscape which brings those prepared to explore it on foot as close to Heaven as you get on Earth." In a famous paean to the dales in his 1928 book, *Four Boon Fellows*, Brown took it even further:-

There must be dales in Paradise,
Which you and I will find,
And walk together dalesman-wise,
And smile (since God is kind)
At all the foreign peoples there
Enchanted by our blessed air!

All in a name

Some of the first 'foreigners' to be enchanted by that bracing, Swaledale air left their mark indelibly on the landscape in the form of the placenames which punctuate the 30-mile length of the dale from Hollow Mill Cross, at its head, to Richmond, where it meets the lowlands of the Vale of Mowbray before finally joining the mighty Ouse at Beningbrough. I'll always remember being completely fascinated hearing the famous Dales scholar and historian Dr Arthur Raistrick say that by just listening to a Dalesman's accent, he could not only tell which *dale* he came from, but which *part* of the dale.

The lower parts of the dales, including Swaledale, are littered with placenames given by Danish settlers, typically ending in the suffix 'by,' such as Skeeby, Easby, Melsonby and Kirkby Hill, around Richmond. The middle reaches of the dale were settled by Anglian people, from the Low Countries around the Baltic Sea. They were the ones who made the first major forest clearances, and the names of their settlements typically end in 'ley' (which indicates a clearing), such as Healaugh, which means 'high clearing'.

Some of the most noticeable Anglian placenames in Middle and Upper Swaledale are those which include that *gehaeg* element, meaning 'a hedged enclosure.' According to archaeologist Andrew Fleming in his fine book *Swaledale – Valley of the Wild River* (1998), names with this element indicate the late clearance of woodland. Examples include Cringley, Brownsey, Whitaside and Harkerside, which originally meant 'the deer enclosure.'

Other Anglian settlements include the 'ton' element (which also means an enclosure or homestead), such as Grinton – 'green enclosure'; Ellerton – 'alder enclosure', or Fremington – 'enclosure of Fremi's people.' The name of the 'capital' of Middle Swaledale, Reeth, is also Old English and simply means 'stream' – presumably taken from its position on the Arkle Beck.

The higher, wilder and more open upper parts of the dales were settled by Vikings and Norsemen, who reached the dales from the west from Scotland and Ireland in the 9th to 11th centuries. They left us placenames such as Muker – 'narrow field'; Thwaite – 'a cleared meadow'; Keld – 'a spring', and Gunnerside (formerly Gunnersett) – 'Gunnar's summer pasture', all of which have strong Old Scandinavian or Norse elements.

Arkengarthdale is also pure Old Scandinavian, meaning 'the valley of Arnkell's enclosure.' Arnkell was a common Old Scandinavian name, and Ella Pontefract records the fact that an Arkil, son of Gospatrick, still held the estate just before the Conquest. The dale is well-known for its strange-sounding placenames; Whaw for example, comes from the Old English and means an enclosure for cattle, while the amusing Booze simply means the house by the bow, or curve, of the Arkle or Slei Gill Beck. Despite the name, there's no pub in Booze, by the way, so you'll have to walk the half-mile down Scotty Hill to the CB Arms (named after Oliver Cromwell's doctor and local lead mining magnate, Charles Bathurst) at Langthwaite for a drink.

While we are on the subject of funny names, the now ruinous Crackpot Hall, which commands one of the finest views of the Swale gorge between Keld and Muker, has nothing to do the mental condition of the settler who first chose such an isolated but inspiring spot. It probably refers to a nearby pothole in the limestone, although Ella Pontefract in her charming, 1934 book on the dale, claimed that the children of the farmhouse did have "the madness of the moor" about them.

"The children at Crackpot are untamed like their home," she wrote. "Until they go to school and lose a little of their naturalness they are spirits of the moors, running barefoot among them, clambering like animals over the loose stone walls, which are high and hard to scale on this hill-side."

The names of the fells which enclose the head of Swaledale include many references to the *saetrs* ('seats') or summertime pastures of the Norsemen, such as Lovely Seat, Rogan's Seat, High Seat, Ravenseat and Alderson Seat. Many of the natural features of the dale, even the word dale itself, but also fell, clint, beck and foss are all pure Norse in origin, and a sure sign that these high sheep pastures were first settled by Vikings and Norsemen, who perhaps felt more at home in these isolated communities and empty fellsides. They also bred the typical Dalesman – laconic, lanky, long-nosed and long-striding – just like Arthur Raistrick, in fact.

The name of the river itself is a bit of a mystery, because unlike most Pennine rivers which usually have very ancient British names, the Swale's seems to come from the Old English. It means 'the whirling, rushing river', or 'the wild one,' and is a pretty accurate description of the Swale, which is notorious for its rapid rises and frequent flooding. The upper reaches of the Swale are said to have the steepest gradient of any major English river – about 1 in 160. Several bridges crossing the turbulent waters have been swept away in historic times, and dalesfolk know that the power of the waters of 'the wild one' is never to be underestimated.

On the rocks

The geology of Swaledale is simple, and follows the familiar, regular stepped Yoredale sequence of limestones, topped by the shales and Millstone Grit sandstones on the higher reaches. All the visible rocks you will encounter in Swaledale were laid down during the Carboniferous period, an unimaginable 300 to 350 million years ago.

It's perhaps hard to believe today, when you are battling into the teeth of a bone-chilling gale up to a moorland height like Great Shunner Fell at the head of the dale, that these rocks you are walking over were laid down in a sub-tropical sea. The limestones, which include many visible fossil corals and sea creatures, were laid down in that barmy, tropical Carboniferous sea at a time when Britain was far closer to the Equator than it is today, and therefore the temparatures were much higher.

As the million upon million of tiny sea creatures died, they fell to the seabed and eventually were compressed and hardened by later earth movements into the porous limestones of today. While Swaledale may not boast any of the spectacular limestone features of some of the dales further south, such as Malham Cove, Kilnsey Crag and Gordale Scar, there are still little secret limestone gems like Swinner Gill Kirk, and the charming waterfalls at Kisdon, Wain Wath and Catrake above Muker and Keld, where more resistant limestones have forced the river to tumble over white scars of rock.

Limestone is an exceptional rock because it creates two landscapes – one above and the other below ground – and Swaledale has examples of both. Because rainwater is slightly acidic, it gradually eats into the rock, finding and widening the crevices to create that other, unseen underground world of pot, swallow and shake holes, where streams disappear under the moorgrass. Again, Swaledale has no tourist showcaves like those of Wharfedale and Ribblesdale, but a look at the OS map shows the upper pastures to be riddled with these shake or swallow holes, which are usually found where the streams rushing off the millstone grit hit, and are literally swallowed up by, the thirsty limestone.

A rock pool with the peat-stained Wain Wath waterfall in the background.

W. H. Auden famously extolled the merits of a Dales limestone landscape in his poem *In Praise of Limestone*:

> *...Mark these rounded slopes with their surface fragrance of thyme and, beneath,*
> *A secret system of caves and conduits: hear the springs*
> *That spurt out everywhere with a chuckle,*
> *Each filling a private pool for fish and carving*
> *Its own little ravine whose cliffs entertain*
> *The butterfly and the lizard...*

Lead miners pursued these streams to find the galena, or lead ore, which was formed when molten minerals rushing up through the limestone from the depths of the earth solidified into the precious blue-black veins running through the rock. And they created their own industrial landscapes in places like Gunnerside Gill and Old Gang Beck, where side streams were dammed to create a head of water, and then released in what were known as 'hushes' (perhaps the name came from the sound of the rushing water) to scour and excavate the rocks beneath.

The shales and Millstone Grit were laid down on top of the limestones later in the Carboniferous period, as mighty rivers flowing from the north deposited huge sandbanks and muddy deltas which spread over and covered the former seabed. The millstone grit series obviously gets its name from the use to which the hard, abrasive rock, was formerly put – the making of mill and grindstones for mills and forges throughout the country.

The millstone grit-based moorland is much less well-drained than the limestone, hence the notorious peat bogs and heathers of the tops. This is the home of moorland birds like the red grouse, curlew and golden plover; the rucksack-bearing human 'bogtrotter', and the ubiquitous, hardy, white-nosed and curly-horned Swaledale sheep, which originated in the dale and is now found all over the Pennines and even further afield.

The final architects who put the finishing touches to Swaledale's landscape were the great glaciers of the last Ice Age, which swept through the valley carving out its distinctive U shape. It's hard to imagine the crushing, grinding power of these enormous rivers of ice, which only finished their work 10,000 years ago – a mere blink in geological time. Those Ice Age glaciers also left behind distinctive, rounded moraines of glacial debris, seen to good effect at the end of the dale around Hudswell, to the west of Richmond.

Life in the dale

Agriculture is still the main industry in Swaledale as it has been for thousands of years, but tourism has become increasingly important recently and many farmers – or their wives – now also run bed-and-breakfast holiday accommodation as well.

The age-old cycle of life and death, seed time and harvest, still continues as it has since those first Viking and Norse settlers came to the dale a millennium ago. The shepherds still care for their flocks of hardy "Swaddle" sheep, bringing them down from the fells for lambing in the spring, shearing them in summer, and generally keeping an eye on them on those summer pastures the Norse knew as '*saetrs.*' The noble head of a Swaledale tup (ram) was chosen as the highly-appropriate logo for the Yorkshire Dales National Park when it was designated in 1954.

Farmers are encouraged now by grants from Natural England and the National Park to keep their traditional, herb and wildflower-rich hay meadows in the valley bottom, producing the sweet-smelling hay which will not only keep their stock through the winter, but keep the landscape we know and love. And of course there is a bonus in birds, butterflies and other wildlife as a result.

As mentioned before, the true Dales family leads a fairly solitary existence, living in an isolated farmstead often miles from the nearest neighbour or civilisation. They are hardy, independent people who keep themselves to themselves, and are usually quite happy with their own company.

Quite often, the only time they meet up with their neighbours or with farmers from further afield is at the annual sheep sales or local shows. For this reason, these events are as important socially as they are for the buying and selling of stock, and the farmers and their families look forward to them with eager anticipation.

So events like the Tan Hill Sheep Sales, held every May outside the highest pub in the country just across the watershed at the head of West Stone Dale, north of Keld; the Swaledale Agricultural Show (formerly the Muker Tup Show and Fair) in September, and the Reeth Show held in August, have become red letter days in the Swaledale calendar.

The critical eyes of the judges in the sheep and cattle classes and the flower and vegetable shows are watched intently by dalesfolk, and are often the subject of comment for months, sometimes years, afterwards. In the background, the gentle oomp-pah-pah of the local brass band adds atmosphere to a wonderfully warm and convivial occasion, as Mike Kipling's photographs in this book show so vividly.

The Yukon of Yorkshire

A mere century ago, Swaledale might well have been known as 'the Yukon of Yorkshire.' At the height of the 'lead rush' in the 1880s, more than 4,000 miners were employed in the frantic search for the glistening, blue-grey gold of galena in literally scores of mines under these now quiet hills.

The lead was in great demand for the roofing and plumbing of the thousands of civic and commercial buildings which were springing up in the booming days of Empire, and large sums of money were to be made – up to £60,000 a year by one mine – by landowners like the Dukes of Devonshire, the Wharton family, and the Bathurst family from Arkengarthdale. Britain was for many decades the world's biggest exporter of lead, which was also used for printers' type, lead shot and pewter wares.

The history of lead mining in the Pennines goes back to Roman times, and there is a persistent legend that the Romans enslaved native Brigantians in lead mining penal colonies at Hurst, in Swaledale. Whether this is true or not, pigs (ingots) of lead have been found near Hurst bearing the names of Roman emperors including Trajan and Hadrian, which prompts the intriguing prospect that Swaledale lead may have lined the roof of some of Imperial Rome's buildings.

Many of the technical terms used by lead miners have Norse roots, as Arthur Raistrick has pointed out. The common North Country word for a mine, 'a groove,' for example, comes from an Old Norse word meaning 'to dig.' And the high, windy hills where the lead was smelted are called bails or boles, from the Old Norse *bál*, meaning a fire or beacon.

The lead mines of Swaledale were an important part of William the Conqueror's spoils which he handed out to favoured landowners like Earl Rufus of Richmond, and the great Yorkshire abbeys and priories, such as those at Easby, Ellerton and Marrick. The Benedictine priory of Marrick, which now acts as the parish church of St Andrew, was founded between 1154-81 by Roger de Aske, and on the dissolution it was important enough to have a prioress and 12 nuns, while its twin downstream across the river at Ellerton (now in private hands) was a Cistercian foundation.

At the dissolution of the monasteries, King Henry VIII granted the monastic manors of Swaledale to his favourites, who included Thomas Wharton, the founder of a family which was to play a major role in the development of lead mining in the dale.

An abstract pattern of barns and walls.

John Leland, writing in the 1540s, noted that: "The men of Sualdale (Swaledale) be much usid in digging Leade Owre from the great hills on each side of Sualdale." In those early days, most of the mines in Swaledale were bell pits – vertical shafts which were sunk to meet the lead vein, and then extended sideways to follow it. The fellsides of Swaledale and Arkengarthdale are covered in these collapsed bell pits, typically surrounded by circular spoils tips and running in straight lines along the hillside. They are dangerous places, however, and should be approached with caution. Later, levels or adits were driven into the hillsides in both Swaledale and Arkengarthdale, where natural, steep-sided gills cut across the veins, and smelt mills, such as Charles Bathurst's curious octagonal building in Arkengarthdale, chimneys, crushing wheels and dressing floors were built alongside the mines.

'Hushing', as described earlier, was another common early mining technique, used to get at the veins of lead ore where they were associated with steep slopes and running becks. The lunar landscape in the upper reaches of Gunnerside Gill, or on the Old Gang Levels above Surrender Bridge, shows the size and extent of repeated hushing, where the huge rocky gullies created by the activity are so large that they look almost natural.

A large stretch of the eastern bank of Gunnerside Gill is taken up by three enormous hushes – known as Bunton, Friarfold and Gorton – while opposite on the western bank, the equally spectacular North Hush runs down from the Lownathwaite Mines. Because of the high amounts of lead contamination left in the soil, no vegetation will grow in these unnatural gullies. It is an industrialised landscape on an colossal scale, and often comes as a bit of a shock for many people who have only seen the dale from the roadside.

The North Rake Hush in neighbouring Mill Gill, or Old Gang Beck, upstream from Surrender Bridge on the Feetham-Arkengarthdale road, are other good examples, and more prominent hushes are to be seen around Slei Gill in Arkengarthdale. The old mine buildings here, at the Old Gang Mines and in Gunnerside Gill, now mostly protected as Scheduled Ancient Monuments, remain as silent reminders of the days when Swaledale echoed with the sounds and sights of industry.

Until the 17th century, lead prospectors in Swaledale and Arkengarthdale were generally allowed free access to the then-unenclosed fellside in their search for the precious ore. If they struck lucky, they would stake their claim and have the first option to mine the lead. Landowners would claim a royalty of between an eighth and a twelfth of the value of any ore discovered, but later they took a more active role by supplying the venture capital for more ambitious, and productive, mines.

Mining companies such as the CB Company in Arkengarthdale and the Quaker-inspired London Lead Company gradually took over the larger mines, and although working conditions were always harsh, for the most part, they tried to look after their workers through the many depressions which hit the industry.

Lead mining was always a difficult, dirty and dangerous job, as T.D.Whitaker observed in his *History of Richmondshire* (1823):

"In Swaledale and the adjoining districts, where mining prevails, habits of subterranean toil and danger, together with seclusion from light and society, while they harden the constitution in general, steel the nerves, and necessarily produce a degree of ferocity very formidable when highly excited. In the mining villages only of Richmondshire are to be found those appearances of squalid neglect about the persons of the inhabitants, and those external accumilations of domestic filth about their dwellings, which sicken every stranger in the worst parts of Lancashire and the West Riding of Yorkshire."

By the end of the 19th century, the lead boom was over, and by the time Queen Victoria died, it was in terminal decline. Cheaper foreign imports signalled the end, and many miners emigrated to Durham and Lancashire to find work. In 1851, Arkengarthdale boasted a population of 1,283, but it has dwindled ever since. Melbacks, the parish which included a number of Swaledale's mining fields, had 1,661 inhabitants in 1851; today it numbers about 300. Between the censuses of 1891 and 1971, the population of Swaledale halved.

Regal Richmond

Edmund Bogg, that aptly-named and effusive Edwardian chronicler of the northern moors, was obviously in love with Richmond, the 'capital' of Swaledale and according to no less an authority than Alec Clifton-Taylor, one of the finest of English country towns.

In his *Regal Richmond and the Land of the Swale* published in 1909, Bogg described how approaching the town on foot: "The growing propinquity to such a natural stronghold, more like some fortress town on the Rhine, excites rather than wearies the pedestrian." And he added: "If one might give it a descriptive title, worthy of its majesty and charm, it is the Yorkshire Heidelberg!"

While Richmond cannot quite claim to be the home of English Romanticism and one of the oldest universities in Europe (nor the inspiration for Romberg's ever-popular operetta *The Student Prince*, also based on Heidelberg), it nevertheless exerts a strong, economic and cultural influence on Swaledale and the surrounding countryside. And in Bogg's defence, it has to be said that Richmond Castle, high on its crag above the Swale, bears more than a passing resemblance to Heidelberg's Gothic and Renaissance castle above the Neckar (not, incidentally, the Rhine as Bogg supposed).

Founded by the Norman Earl, Alan Rufus shortly after the Conquest in 1071, the town grew up around his castle, built on the *riche-mont* or 'strong hill' on its crag above the River Swale, which gave the town its name. The name is thought to have come originally from Rufus's home in Brittany.

In the mid 12th century, Conan "the Little" Earl of Richmond and Duke of Brittany, added the Great Keep, which was finished by Henry II, and the curtain and town walls were added. The imposing castle was never besieged, and in 1174 it was used to imprison the Scottish King, William the Lion.

One of the legends attached to Richmond Castle, gleefully recounted by Bogg, is that in a secret vault deep in the rock beneath the foundations of the castle, King Arthur and his fabled Knights of the Round Table lie sleeping, waiting for the call to come to the nation's rescue. He tells the tale of Potter Thompson, who accidentally happened upon the cave, only to drop Excalibar and flee the cave in terror. It's a familiar story, also told of Lliwedd in Snowdonia and Housesteads Crag in Northumberland, and is a common folktale linked to the Once and Future King.

Nowadays, the only soldiers you will see in Richmond will be squaddies from the nearby Catterick Barracks, one of the largest Army camps in the country, whose genesis was here in Richmond. The founder of the Scouting Movement, Lord Robert Baden Powell, planned the camp when he was Commanding Officer of the Northern Division of the Territorial Army, and living in Richmond Barracks inside the castle between 1908-1910. The camp eventually opened in 1915.

Richmond assumed its present role as an important regional centre for the dale and surrounding countryside in the medieval period, when it became a chartered borough and royal charters were granted giving it the right to hold markets and fairs. At this time, the town had no less than 13 craft guilds controlling its trade, and amazingly, two still exist today. Henry IV granted Richmond the royal charter which gave it the right to hold a market in 1441, and the street market is still held in one of the largest cobbled market places in England taking place every Saturday, in the shadow of the former Church of the Holy Trinity (now the Regimental Museum of the Green Howards and until 1971 lined by shops beneath its north aisle) and watched over by the castle keep.

The late 17th and 18th centuries marked Richmond's fashionable heyday. The Georgian period was one of great prosperity for the town when fine new houses and buildings replaced many of the older medieval buildings. Frenchgate and Newbiggin still have some of the finest Georgian streetscapes in the country, and many other houses built at this time surrounded the cobbled Market Place, including the Town Hall, which was built as an Assembly Room in 1756.

Well-to-do families came to Richmond from all over the country to attend the horse racing which took place on the Race Course, and assemblies, card parties and military musters were among the other social attractions. The King's Head Hotel, built in 1718 for the Bathurst family from Arkengarthdale, was the main accommodation for these wealthy tourists, and it still stands overlooking the Market Place.

But perhaps the finest Georgian survival in Richmond is its charming little theatre in Friar's Wynd, opposite the Grey Friar's Tower, all that remains of a Francescan Friary. The tiny theatre was founded in 1788 by the grandly-named Tryphosa Brockell, a travelling player from Barnard Castle, whose third husband, a staymaker from York, managed the theatre in its early days. After a long period of decay, it was lovingly restored to regular theatrical use in 1963, and has been subject to further restoration since. It is one of the smallest, oldest but most intimate theatres in the country, and seats only about 240 people in the original seats and galleries. But it is a theatrical experience not to be missed.

The York, Newcastle and Berwick Railway reached Richmond in a branch line from Eryholme in 1846, and in addition to serving as the outlet for much of Swaledale's lead ore to other parts of the country, the railway and its gabled station also opened up the wonders of Swaledale to the growing band of tourists from the south. The line closed in 1968 and the former station building, designed in Tudor style by architect G T Andrews, and now listed as Grade II*, has recently been tastefully converted to a two-screen community cinema, café, restaurant, art gallery and heritage centre, now known simply as The Station.

Richmond, incidentally, is the source of all the 57 other Richmonds throughout the world, including the more famous London one with its splendid Park. And that famous song, *Sweet Lass of Richmond Hill*, was composed by Leonard McNally for his wife, the former Frances I'Anson, who was born in Leyburn, Wensleydale, but was associated with Hill House, Richmond, through her maternal grandparents.

So Swaledale's influence and fame continues to echo around the world. But when Ella Pontefract called Swaledale "a little country in itself", she summed up the 'dale of the wild river' perfectly.

Bluebells in a wildflower meadow near Thwaite.

Regal Richmond

Banks of frothy cow parsley form the foreground to this distant view of Richmond castle and town.

Conan, Earl of Richmond's four-square keep still dominates the pantiled roofs and jumbled cottages of Richmond as it has for over nine centuries, in this view of the town as seen from the west.

A fine view of Richmond from Maison Dieu, watched over by the keep and curtain walls of the castle, with the start of Swaledale in the distance.

Another view from Maison Dieu, showing the tower of Trinity Church and the Market Place.

This misty view of the castle keep standing watch over the silvery Swale from Maison Dieu seems to add credence to the legend of King Arthur and his Knights who allegedly lie sleeping in a cave beneath the castle.

A bowls match in progress provides the foreground to this view of the castle and town.

Another view from Easby, showing the way that the castle keep, highlighted by sunshine, dominates the town.

An view of Richmond, dominated by its castle, from Easby to the south east.

Simple redbrick Georgian elegance in Bargate.

A study in red and white simplicity – a cottage on the hill in Bargate.

Springtime comes to a cottage on The Green, Richmond.

A wintry view of Richmond, seen after a light fall of snow.

Most people will enter Richmond over the medieval Green Bridge, which has spanned the Swale for centuries. Built in 1788 by John Carr it is so named because it crosses the river to Richmond Green.

23

right

It had just gone 11.30am when Mike Kipling captured this beautiful detail of an 18th century sundial on the corner of a house on Bridge Street. The Latin inscription, freely translated, means "So the hours, such is life." It was erected by William Hutton in 1720.

far right

A year later, William Hutton was responsible for the erection another sundial, this time on The Green side of the same house.

The Howard Room in the Museum of the Green Howards in the former Church of the Holy Trinity, in Richmond Market Place. It commemorates the Howard family, founders of the regiment.

The Medal Room in the museum, contains over 3000 medals, including 18 Victoria Crosses won by members of the Regiment over 150 years.

Culloden Tower, a mock-Gothic 'eye-catcher' above the Swale at Hudswell, west of Richmond, was erected on the site of an old defensive tower known as Hudswell Peele, built to commemorate the victory of the Duke of Cumberland over Bonnie Prince Charle's Jacobites in 1746.

When it's not Market Day, the
Market Place is used as a car park.

The Obelisk and castle keep,
proudly flying the flag of English
Heritage, from the Market Square.

Another view of Richmond Market Place with the Saturday street market in full swing.

The audience's view of the interior of Richmond's unique Georgian Theatre, which was comprehensively restored in 2004.

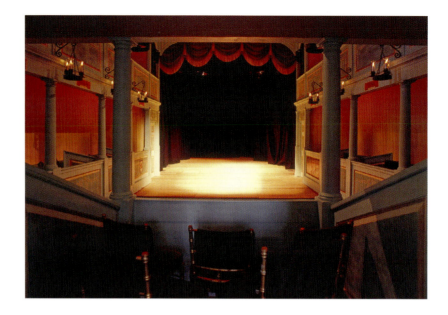

This is the actor's view from the stage of the tiny, yet opulent, theatre.

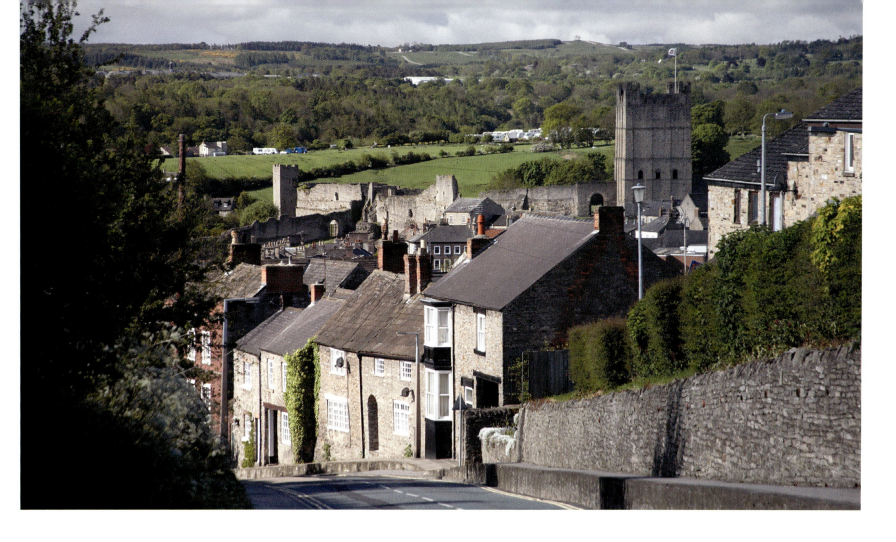

Gallowgate is a steep street which runs down towards the Castle and Market Place. It originally linked to Frenchgate and takes its name from a former gate in the town walls where presumably a gallows once stood.

Frenchgate is another of Richmond's streets running steeply up from the Market Place. It's a stiff pull for a cyclist.

Even when the weather's bad you can still get your vegetables from Richmond market, thanks to the Indoor Market in the Market Place.

A detail of an elegant Georgian doorway, completed with portico and Ionic columns, also in Frenchgate.

A rainbow bisects the 18th century obelisk which stands in the middle of Richmond's cobbled Market Place, on the site of the town's medieval Market Cross.

The view west from the keep into the jaws of Swaledale, with the Culloden Tower in the left middle distance.

Another rainbow arches over the castle keep in this view from the courtyard.

The 15th century parish church of St Mary's (right) seen from across the Market Place from the castle.

The Market Place and the former Holy Trinity Church seen from the castle keep.

An almost aerial view of the Culloden Tower seen from across the town from the castle keep.

The interior of the converted railway station, now known simply as The Station.

Richmond's Tudor-style railway
station has recently been converted
to a heritage centre, community
cinema and restaurant by a group
of dedicated local people.

Strong morning sunlight lights the
battlements of Richmond Castle,
in this view from the south.

Earl Conan's mighty castle keep
from the courtyard.

The castle framed by the arch of the Green Bridge over the River Swale.

The River Swale lives up to its reputation as 'the wild one' beneath the town of Richmond.

The Swaledale scene: a journey up the dale

Muker – the Norse name means 'narrow field' – lies at the junction of the Swale and the Straw Beck, which flows down from Great Shunner Fell, seen on the far right horizon in this picture taken from the north bank of the Swale.

Haymaking patterns near Ellerton Lodge in lower Swaledale.

The elegant bell tower of the stable block at Marske Hall, on the old road between Richmond and Reeth, is topped by a cupola, as seen in this distant view.

The remains of Ellerton Priory lie a mile away on the opposite bank of the Swale to Marrick. Sheltered by a spreading yew tree, the remains consist mainly of the battlemented tower of this priory, which was run by nuns of the Cistercian order.

A shaft of sunlight illuminates the tower of Marrick Priory, on the banks of the Swale east of Grinton, with Garnless Scar above. The priory was founded for Benedictine nuns in the 12th century by Roger de Aske.

A panoramic view from Harkerside of Reeth, the 'capital' and the largest village in Swaledale.

The mock-medieval battlemented tower of Grinton Lodge Youth Hostel was the author's introduction to Swaledale. A former shooting lodge, it stands high above the village on Hirst Ridge, an outlier of Grinton Moor.

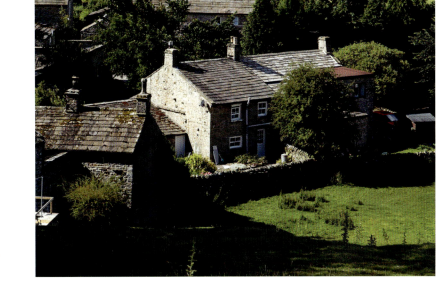

There are two Fremingtons in Swaledale – High and Low. The twin villages lie between Grinton and Reeth, just above the flood plain of the Swale. This is Low Fremington seen from High Fremington.

The bay-fronted village Post Office
at Reeth.

The Black Bull Hotel (traditonally painted
white) on the green at Reeth is the village's
most famous hostelry.

A fine black and white detailed Georgian door in Reeth.

A peep down a ginnel towards the village green in Reeth, with scars of limestone on Fremington Edge beyond.

Stormy skies threaten over wind-tossed
cow parsley and buttercups in this summer
view between Reeth and Healaugh.

Sunlight puts the spotlight on the village of Healaugh between Reeth and Gunnerside in mid-Swaledale.

Healaugh from Harkerside,
with Calver Hill towering in
the background.

A bank of daffodils fronts
this traditional gritstone cottage
in Healaugh.

Low Row, between Healaugh and Gunnerside in mid-Swaledale, is what is known as a linear village – that is, it stretches along one street.

Bridges over the Swale have to be sturdy affairs to withstand the winter floods, and this one at Scabba Wath, near Healaugh, is no exception. It occupies a fording point on the old Roman road between Bainbridge and Greta Bridge.

Low Row seems to live up to its name when seen here from a buttercup-covered roadside verge.

An isolated farm near the village of Low Row.

The essence of Swaledale – blooming heather in the foreground, and a glorious view looking west into the heart of the sofly wooded dale. The scene from High Lane, above Feetham.

A typical field barn, surrounded by wild flower meadows, at Banks Heads near Crackpot.

The view down the dale from above the hamlet of Crackpot in mid-Swaledale.

This clock was unveiled in 2000 in the centre of Gunnerside to mark the Millennium.

Gunnerside lies at the heart of Swaledale on the northern bank of the river. It is a village once famous for its lead mines.

Gritstone slate roofs
in Gunnerside.

Another study in stone slates, with
the typical Dales fields-and-barns
landscape beyond.

Time was when every village in the
country had its blacksmith's shop.
But today, to find the Old Working
Smithy in Gunnerside is a rarity and
a poignant reminder of the past.

A smart estate agent would call
this outside lavatory a 'gardener's
toilet', but in Gunnerside,
it's simply known as a 'netty'.

The flood meadows nearest the River Swale at Gunnerside are known as Gunnerside Bottoms.

Emerald fields at Gunnerside Bottoms in spring.

The scene is transformed in winter, when the drystone walls surrounding the village stand out against the snow like lines on a blank sheet of paper.

previous pages
The 'one barn to every two fields' rule is seen to good effect at Gunnerside Bottoms.

Gunnerside, framed by the branches of an ash tree. Gunnerside Gill leads off in the background.

The hamlet of Ivelet lies on a minor road between Gunnerside and Muker.

Crow Trees Farm, near Muker,
is a typical farmhouse/livestock
barn Pennine longhouse. It stands
near the steep descent down
Oxnop Gill on the minor road
between Swaledale and Askrigg,
in Wensleydale.

The view from Crow Trees looking up the
dale on a fine summer's day.

A restored farmhouse and barn at Oxnop,
near Muker.

Oxnop Scar frowns down on
the edge of Satron Moor above
Oxnop Gill on the Askrigg road.

The tower of Muker's parish church
looks over this fine Georgian house
in the village's main street.

Calvert Houses Farm is on
the north bank of the Swale,
near Muker, and stands beneath
Cock Crow Scar.

The centre of Muker, with the tower of the parish church watching over the village.

A typical field-and-barn landscape near Muker.

Early evening shadows lengthen in this distant view of Muker.

Muker seems to sit like a spider in the centre
of a web of drystone walls in this photograph.

A charming waterfall in
Upper Swaledale.

The essence of Swaledale:
a herb-rich wildflower meadow,
drystone walls, and a field barn.
This photograph was taken
near Muker.

Interesting summer cloud formations seen from Crackpot Hall.

The old cast-iron range at Crackpot
Hall has seen better days.

Barn, trees and shadows from
Crackpot Hall.

Fields and barns around Keld.

A typical Swaledale scene,
photographed above Keld.

Keld – the appropriate name is Scandinavian and means 'spring' – is the last and highest village in Swaledale, and it is the centre of the dale's 'Waterfall Country.'

A bright red telephone box and yellow daffodils
add vivid colour to this springtime view of Keld.

The centre of Keld village. Note the
bell-cote and sun-dial (dated 1840)
on the two-storey porch on the
Congregational chapel in the centre.

A glorious summer view of Upper
Swaledale near Keld.

Keld marks a very special crossroads on the walkers' map of England, as it is exactly half-way along Alfred Wainwright's Coast to Coast Walk, and the the footbridge over the River Swale is where it crosses Tom Stephenson's Pennine Way. These walkers are resting above Kisdon Force.

An isolated barn near Keld.

Eddies form fascinating patterns
below East Gill Force.

Kisdon Force is the biggest and best-known of the many waterfalls in the upper reaches of the Swale. As the river emerges from a narrow gorge, it plunges 10 feet/ three metres into a large pool, seen here.

It then cascades over three limestone terraces and into a narrow trough.

East Gill Force lies just below the village of Keld, where the stream enters the Swale via a series of cascades.

The leafy scene from the brink of Catrake Force.

Wain Wath Force, near Keld, is in the very highest reaches of the River Swale, and in winter takes on a fairytale appearance...

... but in summer, the view is entirely different. The name means 'wagon ford', and the river here is quite shallow as it flows over broad shelves of limestone.

More cascading waterfalls in Cliff Beck.

The name of Thwaite gives away the origin of this Upper Swaledale village. It comes from the Old Norse and means 'a clearing'. This photograph shows the village bridge.

Another view of the grey stone village of Thwaite.

The village clusters around the Thwaite Beck.

Winter snows blanket this view of Thwaite.

Swaledale sheep are renowned for their hardiness, and this winter view near Thwaite shows exactly why it is such a useful characteristic.

The Buttertubs Pass, seen here in winter, is the highest point of the Muker to Hawes (or Cliff Gate) road at the head of Swaledale. It gets its name from the strange, fluted columns of limestone in the foreground, which resemble the tubs which were used to churn butter.

The view from the head of a snowy Swaledale from Cliff Gate Road, the minor road which links Swaledale to Hawes in Wensleydale.

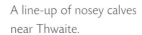
A line-up of nosey calves near Thwaite.

Buttercups, bluebells and meadow cranesbill provide a dainty foreground frieze to this picture of a haymeadow near Thwaite.

The classic shot of Upper Swaledale, looking south from Thwaite, with the flanks of Kisdon Hill rising to the left.

This pyramidical cairn was erected by Muker Parish Council at Green Side, on Cliff Gate Road, the minor road to Hawes, to mark the millennium.

Cliff Gate Road is popular with motorcyclists, but it was all too much for this fellow, who was caught taking a nap by the Millennium Cairn.

These ramblers are enjoying
a well-earned pint outside
the Tan Hill Inn.

91

"Was it chicken or lamb you ordered...?"

The Tan Hill Inn, at 1,732 feet / 530 metres above the sea on Stonesdale Moor north of Keld, is the highest pub in England.

Arkengarthdale

Langthwaite, the main settlement in Arkengarthdale, clusters around its trim village green, in this unusual view taken from the hills above the village.

The hamlet of Whaw (the strange name comes from the Old English and means an enclosure for cattle), straddles the Arkle Beck by Whaw Bridge, in Arkengarthdale.

Scar House is a stately, gabled Victorian former shooting lodge on Scarhouse Lane beneath Low Moor, just north of Langthwaite in Arkengarthdale.

The 'CB' Inn at Langthwaite in Arkengarthdale is a popular meeting place for both local residents and visitors. It is named after Charles Bathurst, a 19th century lead mining magnate.

Hardy Swaledale sheep form the foreground to this view in Arkengarthdale, with a typical Pennine longhouse in the middle distance.

Winter snow plasters this solitary group of trees in Arkengarthdale.

A stone barn receives the same treatment, pebble-dashed by the driven snow.

Vivid sunlight spotlights the limestone scar of Fremlington Edge in Arkengarthdale, just north of Reeth. The stepped appearance of the scar is typical of the Yoredale series.

A close-up of the longhouse; study gritstone walls and slates, rusting farmgate on the left. The first winter snows powder the rushes in the foreground and the hills beyond.

Some people regret the conversion of old buildings to modern residential use, as is the case with this same longhouse as in the image above. But the alternative – dereliction and eventual ruin – is surely worse.

A lone tractor (left middle distance) makes its steady way from an Arkengarthdale farm as winter starts to take hold on the fells above.

The same scene a few weeks later,
as the snows have descended lower
now to blanket the lower reaches
of the dale.

Showtime in Swaledale

The critical eye of the well-waterproofed judge is cast over this line-up of young Swaledale tups at the annual Swaledale Agricultural Society's show at Muker.

This shepherd's craggy face could surely be that of a Viking.

This is what it's all about – the coveted red winner's rosette adorns a pen of Swaledale tups.

Not a bad day at the show: one first and two seconds.

They start 'em young
in Swaledale. A young
contestant with his ram
at the Muker show.

And it's not just youngsters who exhibit at the show. This young lady was just as keen to win with her tup.

A last anxious look at the curly-horned head of a Swaledale tup before the judges arrive.

"It's good, but I've seen better..."

The quizzical, critical and seasoned eye of the judge at the Muker show. Note the waterproof overtrousers and the Swaledale Sheep Society tie.

The spectators are just as critical as the judges at the Muker show.

"Just hold him steady while
I take a good look."

The line up of young Swaledale
tups faces the judges.

"Yes, but is it straight?" The judge in the sheep crook class lines up a possible winner.

The skill of carving sheep crooks and walking sticks from rams' horns has been developed to a fine art in the Dales. This selection includes representations of a pheasant, sheep-dog at work, and leaping salmon.

Pickles, chutneys, jams and wines – all go before the judges' critical eyes in the horticultural tent.

The judge sets to work on the vegetable classes.

A general shot inside the horticultural show tent at the Muker show.

Providing a musical backdrop to events at the show is the Muker Silver Band, seen here in full flight.

The cornets are usually the tune-carriers of the band...

...while the trombones give that deep warmth to the sound...

...aided by a lady tuba player.

The level of inspection is just as great at the sheep sale as it is at an agricultural show like Muker.

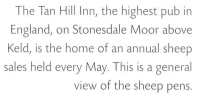

The Tan Hill Inn, the highest pub in England, on Stonesdale Moor above Keld, is the home of an annual sheep sales held every May. This is a general view of the sheep pens.

Local farmers take a closer look at some Swaledale tups.

Some local characters share a joke at the sheep pens.

The lead legacy

The ruinous remains of the former lead Smelting Mill in Old Gang Beck, also known as Mill Gill, above the village of Feetham in mid Swaledale. There are extensive further remains of mines, shafts, tips and hushes in the higher reaches of the beck, which rises on Little Punchard, or Gill Head, Moss.

The tell-tale humps and bumps in these fields near Gunnerside are signs of "t'owd man", as the old lead miners are known in these parts.

The scars of lead mining activities above the village in Gunnerside Gill can clearly be seen in this long view from across the valley.

The entrance to the East Gill lead mine in Gunnerside Gill. Note the huge spoil tip below the entrance.

Inside one of the flues which fed the lead smelters at the Bunton mills.

The 'moonscape' of the Bunton Level lead mining remains in Gunnerside Gill. Bunton is also one of three massive 'hushes' in the gill, where water was impounded and then released to excavate the lead ore.

Another view of the Bunton Levels, showing some of the remaining buildings.

The remaining buildings of the
Sir Francis lead mine on the west
bank of Gunnerside Gill.

Another view of the Sir Francis
lead mine.

Looking out from the fern-draped entrance of the adit to the East Gill mine.

Looking a bit like a Mayan ruin emerging from a South American rainforest, these mighty buttresses are part of the Sir Francis lead mine.

PHOTOGRAPHER'S NOTES
BY MIKE KIPLING

Photography is all about capturing the spirit and emotion of a place through a mixture of light, location and composition. My photographs of Swaledale have been taken over a 10 year period. Some were taken as part of magazine or tourism commissions and some were taken specifically for this book. But most were taken for my own pleasure as a personal project trying to capture the essence of the dale as I first found it in the late 1960s.

Visually, in many respects, not a lot has changed. Much care has been taken not to spoil the fabric of the villages and the town of Richmond. Conservation of landscape and buildings by the National Park Authority has encouraged more wildflower meadows, removed dereliction and brought many traditional threatened buildings back into economic use. All of which has made taking attractive images at times very easy. Parked cars – the landscape and townscape photographers' curse – are a problem and seem to find their way into every open space.

Until three years ago all my photography was on medium format film, using Bronica and Mamiya cameras. Film stock was primarily Fuji Velvia 50 with a few images taken on Fuji Provia 100. With the exception of two snow shots of Arkengarthdale, the only filters used were graduated neutral density and polarisers. When I felt modern professional digital cameras outperformed scanned, medium format film, size for size, I changed to digital. Digital photographs were taken on Canon 1DSMk11 and 5D cameras with L series lenses. Images were shot in Raw format and processed in Adobe Photoshop.